23·70

EVANSTON PUBLIC LIBRARY

T5-CVE-321

3 1192 01183 2416

x598.942 Hauge.H

Haugen, Hayley Mitchell,
1968-
Eagles /

DATE DUE

OCT - 8 2003	
MAY 2 1 2008	

DEMCO, INC. 38-2931

Eagles

EVANSTON PUBLIC LIBRARY
CHILDREN'S DEPARTMENT
1703 ORRINGTON AVENUE
EVANSTON, ILLINOIS 60201

NATURE'S PREDATORS

Hayley Mitchell Haugen

KIDHAVEN PRESS

THOMSON

GALE

Detroit • New York • San Diego • San Francisco
Boston • New Haven, Conn. • Waterville, Maine
London • Munich

Library of Congress Cataloging-in-Publication Data

Haugen, Hayley Mitchell, 1968–
  Eagles / by Hayley Mitchell Haugen.
    p. cm. — (Nature's predators)
  Includes bibliographical references (p.   ).
  Summary: Discusses different kinds of eagles, their physical
characteristics, hunting and feeding methods, as well as the
dangers they face.
    ISBN 0-7377-1004-7 (hardback : alk. paper)
    1. Eagles—Juvenile literature. [1. Eagles. 2. Endangered species.]
  I. Title. II. Series.
  QL696.F32 H38 2002
  598.9'42—dc21

2001007307

Copyright 2002 by KidHaven Press,
an imprint of The Gale Group
10911 Technology Place, San Diego, CA 92127

No part of this book may be reproduced or used in any other form or
by any other means, electrical, mechanical, or otherwise, including,
but not limited to photocopy, recording, or any information storage
and retrieval system, without prior written permission from the pub-
lisher.

Printed in the U.S.A.

Contents

Chapter 1

Eagles Are Predators

E agles belong to a large group of birds called **raptors**, or **birds of prey**. As their name suggests, these birds are **predators**; they hunt and kill other animals for survival. Eagles belong to the order of raptors called Falconiformes. Birds in this group hunt during the day and sleep at night.

At least one of the sixty different species of eagles can be found on every continent. They live in deserts and open plains, in jungles and forests, and along the shores of swamps, lakes, and rivers. The various species of eagles can be divided into four groups.

The first group is known as sea eagles or fish eagles. Eagles in this group, such as the American (or bald eagle) in the United States and the Steller's sea eagle of Japan, **roost** near rivers, lakes, and seashores, and they mostly hunt fish. To aid them in fishing over water, they have no feathers below the knee to get wet when they

Eagles' Ranges

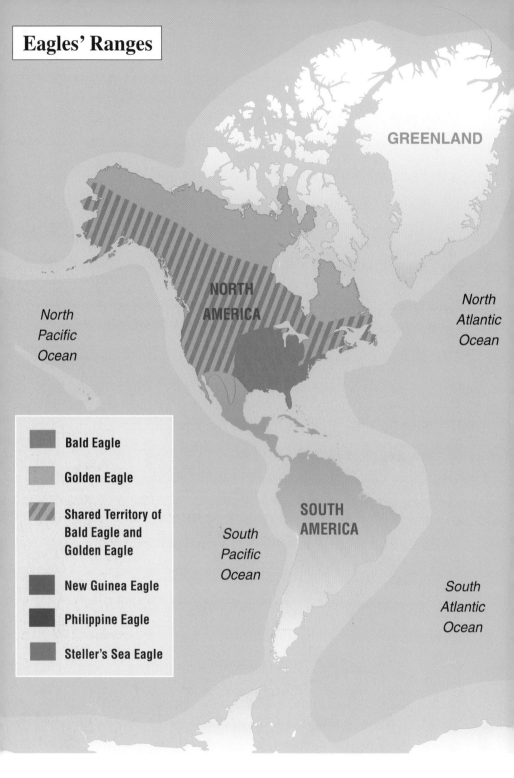

GREENLAND

NORTH AMERICA

North Pacific Ocean

North Atlantic Ocean

Bald Eagle

Golden Eagle

Shared Territory of Bald Eagle and Golden Eagle

New Guinea Eagle

Philippine Eagle

Steller's Sea Eagle

SOUTH AMERICA

South Pacific Ocean

South Atlantic Ocean

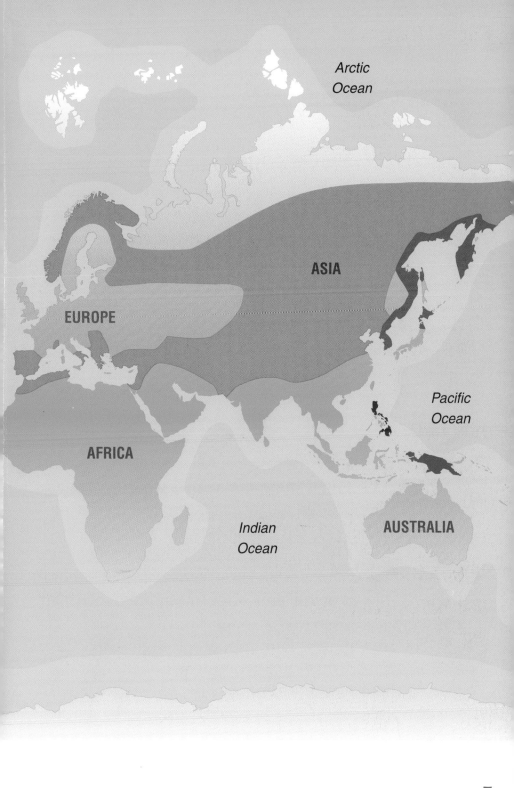

Arctic
Ocean

ASIA

EUROPE

Pacific
Ocean

AFRICA

Indian
Ocean

AUSTRALIA

snag **prey** from the surface of the water. Fish eagles also have sharp, bumpy growths called **spicules** on the bottom of their feet that aid them in holding their wet, slippery prey.

Other Groups of Eagles

The second group of eagles includes the serpent, snake, or harrier eagles. Snake eagles are characterized by large yellow eyes and short, strong toes. These birds, such as the extremely rare Congo and Madagascar serpent eagle, live in deserts or dense tropical jungles, which provide plenty of snakes and other reptiles for them to prey on. In addition to preying on snakes and reptiles, some birds in this group, such as the Bateleur eagle of Africa, also prey on small birds and other mammals. Like most eagles, they also eat dead animals, or **carrion**.

Buzzards or harpies, which belong to the third group of eagles, live in Europe, Asia, South America, and Mexico. The Philippine monkey-eating eagle and the New Guinea harpy eagle also belong to this group. The largest and most powerful of all the raptors, the New Guinea harpy eagle, which can weigh as much as twenty pounds, is known to eat other birds as big as itself and large mammals such as monkeys and sloths.

The last in the four groups of eagles are the booted eagles, which are generally smaller than eagles in the other three groups. Booted eagles have feathers growing on their legs all the way down to their toes, which make them look like they are wearing boots. These birds are found throughout the world in a wide array of habitats, and they eat a large variety of prey.

The golden eagle is one example of a booted eagle and is the most common eagle in the world. In the United States, the golden eagle lives mainly in the mountainous regions of the West, nesting in cliff caves or tall trees and feeding on rabbits and rodents such as ground squirrels or prairie dogs.

Eagles Are Built to Hunt

From the tip of an eagle's sharp, hooked beak, to the points of its deadly claws, almost every part of its body is built to assist it in hunting or eating prey. An eagle's keen vision, varied flying skills, and strong feet and **talons** all work together when it is on the hunt.

Eagles' eyes have many special features that help them hunt. Unlike many other birds, such as parrots, finches, or parakeets, birds of prey have eyes that face forward on their head (like humans), rather than to the sides. This placement provides eagles with binocular, or three dimensional, vision, which allows them to judge depth and distance.

Forward-facing eyes help eagles see great distances.

Eagles, however, can see eight times better than humans. With this powerful eyesight, an eagle can spy a fish in the water from nearly a mile away. In addition to being sharp, an eagle's vision can adjust for reflections on water so that the bird will not lose sight of its prey.

Eagles can also see well to the sides of their head. Because an eagle can turn its head 270 degrees, or three-quarters of a circle around, from a single location, it can survey much of its immediate surroundings for prey.

Finally, eagle eyes also have the additional benefit of being protected by an extra eyelid. Along with their upper and bottom eyelids, each eagle eye contains another clear eyelid. This extra eyelid moves across the eagle's eye sideways, cleaning and moistening it as it moves.

Known as the **nictitating membrane**, the eagle's extra eyelid protects the eye from dust and rain when the bird is flying. It also acts like a pair of sunglasses for the bird, providing a screen to protect the eye from bright sunlight that could hurt the bird's ability to hunt.

Eagles in Flight

An eagle's vision helps it find its prey, but its bone structure and flying abilities allow it to chase down and carry that prey. Birds can fly because their bones are hollow, which makes them very light. Even the skeleton of a large eagle such as the bald eagle weighs only about half a pound. And all of its seven thousand feathers weigh less than one and a half pounds.

Eagle Bone Structure

An eagle spreads its wings in flight. Lightweight, hollow bones help eagles fly fast and high.

In all, most eagles weigh between eight and twenty pounds, but their bones, though hollow, are strong. Eagle bones, for example, are reinforced by cross-ribs, much in the way that a house is supported by extra wooden beams. With this extra support, eagles can carry prey that often weighs as much as they do.

Like its bones, an eagle's feathers are also strong. The hard material that runs down the center of feathers is made up of keratin, the same substance that creates human fingernails. The feathers of eagles and other birds of prey are layered and allow the bird more speed in hunting.

Wing feathers overlap to form a broad kind of fan that pushes air down and back as the bird flies.

An eagle pounces on its prey, its layered feathers visible on the underside of its wing.

Some feathers on the wing can be spread wide like a hand, or lifted to help an eagle control its speed. These actions reduce air resistance that might make the bird stall in midflight and lose an opportunity to catch its prey. Body feathers of eagles are smaller than wing feathers, but they also aid an eagle's flight. These feathers fit together tightly so the bird can glide easily through the air.

The feathers of different types of eagles further aid them in the hunt. For instance, harpy eagles, and other eagles that must hunt in dense forests or tropics, have short wings but long tails to help them move through trees. Eagles that hunt in mountainous regions or open countryside, on the other hand, have long, broad wings stretching up to eight and a half feet wide, which allow for lengthy, effortless flight.

Soaring

While soaring through the air, eagles can reach heights of as much as fourteen thousand feet, and they fly for hundreds of miles each day in search of prey. When flying, however, eagles and other birds of prey are unique because they spend very little time actually flapping their wings. Eagles flap to reach a good height, but because of their large, powerful wings, they can glide in the air for hours. They simply ride the rising hot air currents.

These currents are called **thermal updrafts**. The thermal updrafts allow birds to soar as high as two miles without flapping. This leisurely style of

The eagle's average gliding speed is thirty miles per hour.

---

flying is an advantage to eagles because they can hunt for food in this manner without tiring.

In the air, eagles simply need to focus on steering toward their prey. When **gliding** along on the air currents, an eagle's tail feathers will spread out like a fan. The bird can tilt the tail one way or the other to steer itself through the air at an average speed of about thirty miles per hour.

Once the eagle spots prey on the ground, however, it becomes an acrobat of sorts. While on the hunt, eagles can swoop down on their prey from great heights, diving out of the sky and reaching speeds of up to two hundred miles an hour before surprising its kill.

The Deadly Talons

Although eagles' superb vision and flying skills aid them in their attack on prey, no hunt would be complete without the aid of their deadly, sharp claws. With their strong feet and claws, eagles can catch and kill animals as large as themselves.

Each eagle foot has three toes in front and one in the back that can stretch forward and touch the front toes. Eagles use this back toe much like a thumb to help them grab their prey. At the end of the toes are sharp, curved claws, known as talons. Talons can grow as much as an inch and a half long. They are used to grasp and kill prey by piercing through its side like daggers.

Eagles' feet and talons are adapted to the kind of food they eat. Snake eagles' toes, for instance, are thick and strong, which allow them to firmly cling on to wriggling snakes. Snake eagles' legs are also covered with tough scales. These scales protect the

The eagle uses its long talons to grasp and kill prey.

bird against deadly snakebites. In contrast, the Indian black eagle has unusually long toes and thin talons, which it uses to snatch nests of chicks from trees.

Eagles rely on their keen vision, streamlined body structure, and sharp claws to find and catch their prey, but successful hunting takes much more than that. Eagles also need to set up their **territory** and learn different hunting methods to ensure they will have prey for every meal.

Chapter 2

Eagles on the Hunt

An eagle's eyesight, flying skills, and strong feet and sharp talons all work to help make the bird a fierce predator in the wild. But eagles cannot rely on only their physical characteristics to find their prey. They must also be skilled at establishing their territory, scavenging for food, and perfecting various hunting methods.

Home Is Where the Food Is

Birds of prey are very protective of their territory. This is the area that they have established as their home in the wild. Eagles usually live alone with one mate in their home territories. The bigger the eagle, the larger the territory it needs to hunt food and feed itself, especially if food is scarce. If food is more readily available, a larger population of birds of prey within the area might be found.

To establish their territory, many eagles, such as bald eagles, will claim a nesting site, a breeding space, and a home range where they search for food. The home range stretches at least four to six square miles if prey is plentiful.

While perching in exposed areas such as the very tops of tall trees, rocks, cliffs, and even icebergs, an eagle will stand out in the landscape, making it clear to other birds of prey that the territory has been claimed. If another bird of prey enters a territory already claimed by an eagle, it will be attacked until it retreats. In this way, eagles ensure themselves plenty of space in which to hunt, rest, mate, and raise their young.

An eagle stands out on an iceberg clearly marking its territory.

Scavenge First, Hunt Later

Although eagles may spend up to five hours a day searching for food in their established territory, they do not always have to kill the food they eat. Instead, they scavenge for prey that has already been killed by another animal or has died of natural causes. Bald eagles, for example, often perch beside riverbanks while salmon are spawning, or laying their eggs, in the Pacific Northwest.

Pacific salmon die once their eggs are laid. After the fish have died, bald eagles simply collect the dead salmon from the rivers. The spawning season is one of the few times during the year that bald eagles can be seen hunting in groups. When eagles are actively hunting instead of scavenging, they may choose a number of methods to seek their prey. The methods include **still hunting**, hovering or low-level hunting, and hunting on the wing.

Still Hunting

Rather than flying to look for food, many eagles choose to still hunt. Still hunters perch in tall trees, on cliff ledges, or even on telephone poles to survey their territory for prey. In dense forests or jungles, still hunting is especially useful because eagles do not have the room in these areas to fly without trees obstructing their view of prey.

As one of the largest eagles in the world, the Steller's sea eagle is known for still hunting. Found

A bald eagle surveys the ground below for prey, a method called still hunting.

on the northern Pacific coast of the Soviet Union and in North Korea and Japan, this large eagle lifts from its perch when it spots its prey. Its wings spanning more than eight feet in length, the bird makes a brief pursuit, then swoops down to capture its victim. Steller's sea eagles commonly eat salmon, crabs, and mollusks.

Like other sea eagles, Steller's have scaly feet with small bumps on the toes to prevent slimy fish from squirming from its grasp. In addition to seafood, sea eagles, including bald eagles, also hunt hares, baby seals, foxes, and other birds as large as geese.

Hovering, or Low-Level Hunting

In areas such as deserts or open plains, which do not have a lot of trees or good perches from which eagles can still hunt, eagles often choose the low-level, or hovering, approach to capturing their prey. Using this approach, eagles fly low to the ground in search of food. Like a person treading water in a pool, a hovering eagle does not actually move anywhere. Its wings move in circles to keep it in the air, but the bird does not gain any speed for movement. In this fashion, it is able to keep its head in a single position as it focuses in on its prey.

Hunting on the Wing

Eagles also hunt from up high, which is known as hunting on the wing. When an eagle spots prey from a great height, it swoops down on it, grabs it, and flies away with it, all in one motion if the prey is small. This action is called **stooping**. Eagles can carry prey weighing up to one-third their own weight, but for larger prey, it is sometimes necessary to land, kill it, and collect what they can carry before moving on.

An eagle clutches a fish in its talons after swooping to catch it.

When eagles swoop out of the sky to capture their prey, they use their wings to control their speed. In order to dive out of the sky, they must raise their wings at a sharp angle. This movement allows the air to rush past them as they gain speed in their descent.

As eagles approach their prey, their tail feathers spread out and the wings move forward to act as a kind of brake while the birds grab prey in their talons. Sometimes eagles hunting on the wing in the forest simply fly over the treetops and steal the nests of other birds. They take the nests back to their own roost and eat the other birds' eggs and hatchlings.

Bald eagles often hunt from a height to catch sea birds on the water, swooping in on their prey from more than three hundred feet in the air. After spotting a fish as prey, the bald eagle flies close to the water's surface. It hovers for a brief moment with its magnificent wings spread wide.

Next, it quickly dives downward on its prey, thrusting its outstretched talons in front of itself. The eagle grabs the fish in its claws. With the fish in its grasp, the eagle then tightens its hold, piercing and killing the fish with its deadly talons.

After a successful hunt, an eagle will often fly back to its roost to eat its meal. Here, it will once again make use of its beak and talons to eat its prey. An eagle may also choose to save its prey for later consumption, or it may share it with its young.

A hungry martial eagle prepares to feast on its catch of a monitor lizard.

Chapter 3

How Eagles Kill and Eat Their Prey

Whether still hunting, hovering, or hunting on the wing, once an eagle has captured its prey, it then needs to fly with it to an uninhabited tree where it can eat its meal in peace. If the eagle is not careful, another bird may swoop in and steal its catch from the roost. Eagles that capture prey that is too heavy to fly away with have the additional challenge of protecting their catch on the ground. To do so, the bird will stand on the ground with its wings spread wide over the kill until it can secure enough meat to take back to its nest.

Beaks and Talons Are Helpful Tools

Eagles have no teeth with which to pull apart their prey. They use their sharp beaks and talons instead. The top part of the beak, also called the upper **mandible**, has a hooked tip that overlaps the lower bill. The hook is used to tear prey apart. Using its beak, an eagle shreds and tears food into pieces small enough for it to swallow.

An African fish eagle fends off a scavenging stork.

Whatever an eagle has preyed upon, whether fish or rodent or livestock, its strong feet and talons are used to kill the prey by piercing its body. Like the beak, the talons are also used to pull the food apart.

Dining with Snake Eagles

Snake eagles are especially interesting to watch kill and eat their prey. Snakes are easy to kill because they have frail backbones. After spying a snake in the brush, a snake eagle will swoop down and grab it near its head. Next, the eagle, using its strong feet, quickly breaks the snake's neck and paralyzes it.

Poisonous snakes are not much of a threat to snake eagles. The birds can be killed by snakes only if bitten, but this is rare because snake-eating birds bite off a snake's head after breaking its neck. The eagle then swallows the rest of the snake whole. In addition, snakes cannot bite through the bird's tough feet.

The Crop Is a Handy Storage Pouch

If an eagle kills a large animal, such as a monkey or a sloth, it can store enough food in its **crop** to last a few days. A crop is a pouch that is connected internally to the bird's digestive system and appears as a lump on the eagle's upper breast.

As it is eating, an eagle can direct the food it does not need into the crop for later use. When needed, this food is then regurgitated from the crop back into the bird's mouth. The eagle then reswallows the food for proper digestion or feeds it to its young.

The Pellets

Many birds of prey go to great lengths to prepare their food before they eat it. A hawk, for example, will take a bird it has killed to its favorite spot and pluck out its feathers one by one before it attempts to eat it. Eagles, however, do not pick at their food.

An eagle eats its prey in large chunks without preparing it in any special way. Whatever animal it catches, an eagle will eat bones, fur, feathers, or fish scales all at once with each bite. Eagles are able to eat in this manner because of the way their digestive system is built.

An eagle's stomach works to sort out the food that is swallowed into two parts: parts that are useful and parts that are not. Animal parts that cannot be digested, such as feathers and bones, are regurgitated as small, hard **pellets** about the size of a grown man's pinky finger. The outside of the pellets are covered by the indigestible feathers or fur of an eagle's prey, and the inside of the pellets are the inedible bones.

Feasting on a snow goose, the golden eagle will eat the entire bird, then regurgitate the unused portions as pellets.

Feeding the Eaglets

In addition to feeding themselves, adult eagles also feed their eaglets. For the first six weeks of an eaglet's life, both male and female adult eagles feed it every three or four hours. To do so, they must rip up their prey into tiny pieces the eaglets can digest. By the sixth week, eaglets are able to help their parents out a bit by tearing up the prey they have been given and feeding themselves.

Eaglets eat shredded food brought to them by their parents.

The eaglets are fully grown at four months of age. Although many eagles will stay and be fed by their parents for up to an additional six months after first learning to fly, they are capable of hunting their own prey at this age.

Having survived infancy, the eaglets, when they do leave the nest, face almost no animal predators of their own in the wild. They may live up to forty years if they are able to escape the nonanimal threats to their survival, namely, human predators and the destruction of the environment in which they live.

Chapter 4

Eagles as Prey

Raccoons, snakes, crows, and birds, including eagles, often steal eagle eggs or eaglets from roosts, and adult eagles may be attacked by other raptors or occasionally preyed upon by ground predators such as lions and tigers. But generally speaking, eagles have few natural enemies in the wild. Eagles have, however, fallen victim to hunting and the destruction of their environment through human growth and development.

Eagles Are Hunted by Humans

Although it is illegal to kill eagles in America, eagles are sometimes hunted and killed for their feathers. Native Americans often use eagle feathers in their ceremonies, and eagle feathers are valuable to others as well. Eagle-feather collectors are willing to pay a lot of money for the plumage. A single eagle feather can cost ten dollars. A whole tail worth of feathers can sell for $450.

Others kill eagles because they feel they are pests. Farmers and ranchers often poison eagles

Collectors sometimes pay as much as ten dollars for one eagle feather.

or shoot them because they feel the eagles threaten their calves, lambs, and chickens. Eagles, however, usually prey only on animals if they are already dead or dying.

In fact, many environmental groups eager to protect eagles claim that eagles can even be helpful to farmers and ranchers. Eagles eat the rats and other small animals that could become a nuisance on the farm.

Eagles Are Poisoned by Pesticides and Lead Bullets

Pesticides are another human threat to eagles. Pesticides are used to kill insects on farms, but they can also kill eagles. When pesticides wash into rivers and lakes, they poison the fish and waterfowl that eagles prey on. DDT is one pesticide that killed numerous eagles in America during the 1950s.

After the eagles ate the poisoned prey in rivers, the DDT collected in their bodies and eventually blocked the development of calcium. Calcium is what keeps human bones strong, and it is what makes eggshells thick. The lack of calcium caused eagles' eggs to have much thinner shells than normal eggs.

These shells cracked when the adult birds sat on them to keep them warm, and as a result, the chicks died. In larger doses, insecticides such as DDT (which can still be used as an ingredient in other pesticides in the United States) can kill the adult birds themselves. Adult eagles may also become infertile through pesticide poisoning, meaning they are unable to breed.

In addition to being poisoned unintentionally by humans through the use of pesticides, eagles have also been poisoned by the lead contained in bullets. Eagles are not hunted for sport in America, but an effect of sport hunting does harm them. Hunters who shoot waterfowl, such as

Crops dusted with pesticides and waterfowl poisoned with lead from hunters' gun pellets threaten eagle health.

ducks, often use bullets containing lead in their guns. If hunters cannot retrieve the birds they have shot, it is very likely that the dead birds will be eaten by birds of prey or other predators.

Lead is poisonous. When lead breaks down in a dead duck's system, it poisons the flesh of the duck. Eagles that feed off the infected duck are likewise slowly poisoned, whether they eat the lead or not. Lead shot has been banned in many hunting areas, but it is legal in some states in America.

Eagle Habitat Is Encroached upon or Destroyed to Meet Human Needs

Eagles have been poisoned by human's agricultural progress and sport, and the encroachment of humans on eagle habitat is also a problem. As humans clear the land in wilderness areas to make room for farms and cities, eagle habitat disappears.

Some species of eagles have adapted to human development of their territories. As cities grow around them, eagles roost on telephone wires or tall building ledges and live off what remaining prey they can find. The majority of eagles, however, will not hunt or nest in areas populated by people, so eagle populations in these areas often die out.

Additionally, tropical rain forests are being cleared to provide lumber for the timber industry, livestock grazing areas for the beef industry, or

Although eagles do not normally nest in crowded cities (top), eagles can sometimes be seen perched atop telephone poles in or near cities.

ore and other minerals for the mining industry. In southern Asia, the Philippine monkey-eating eagle is endangered because much of its forest habitat has been cleared away. In the Amazon, the harpy eagle has suffered a similar fate.

Laws and Conservation Efforts Are Helping

Although eagles have suffered at the hands of some humans, many people appreciate the majestic birds and fight for their protection. Some power companies, for example, have built barriers around dangerous power poles to prevent the birds from landing there and electrocuting themselves. Other groups have even built special nesting platforms on power poles located in areas with few trees.

Laws in the United States have also helped protect the bald eagle and golden eagle. In 1940, for example, the Bald Eagle Protection Act was passed in America. This act made it illegal for people to kill or trade parts of bald eagles. Today, hunters, poachers, or farmers who kill eagles may be fined up to $5,000 for the crime. They may even have to serve up to one year in jail for killing the birds.

Eagles have also found protection worldwide through the conservation and rehabilitation efforts of environmental groups and government projects. Wildlife reserves and refuges offer safe habitats in which eagles can hunt and breed

Wildlife habitats provide a safe environment for eagles to live and breed.

An eagle in flight is an awesome sight.

while being viewed and enjoyed by humans. Hawk Mountain in the Appalachian Mountains in the United States and Coto Doñana National Park in Spain are just two of many such reserves.

In addition to wildlife reserves, captive-breeding programs have helped save eagle species that are close to extinction. These programs breed eagles and reintroduce them into the wild. Captive-breeding programs are expensive, however; they have their opponents, and the programs are not always successful.

Laws against killing eagles and efforts to save eagle habitat seem to be the most effective means of protecting eagles that are not already endangered. These approaches give eagles the room to live the lives they were meant to as the magnificent predators of the sky.

Glossary

birds of prey: Birds that kill and eat other animals.

carrion: The dead flesh of an animal.

crop: An internal pouch halfway between an eagle's mouth and stomach that is used to store food to eat later.

gliding: Flying without flapping by riding the air currents.

mandible: The upper or lower part of a bird's beak.

nictitating membrane: An eagle's third, see-through eyelid, which cleans the eyes and protects an eagle's eyes from dust, rain, sun, and other dangers.

pellet: A small, solid ball of indigestible food matter that eagles vomit up.

pesticide: A poisonous chemical used to kill insects or other plant and animal pests.

predators: Animals that hunt and kill other animals.

prey: The animals that are hunted and eaten by other animals.

raptors: Birds of prey that hunt their food during the day.

roost: An eagle's favorite perching spot, where it returns at night to sleep.

spicules: The sharp, bumpy growths on the bottom of fish eagles' feet that aid them in holding on to their slippery prey.

still hunting: Hunting for prey from a high perch.

stooping: Surprising prey by dropping down on it suddenly with talons extended for the kill.

talons: Large claws.

territory: The area of land that an animal has claimed for itself in which to hunt, live, and breed.

thermal updraft: An upward current of warm air formed by wind blowing against a cliff or hillside.

For Further Exploration

Jill Bailey, *Birds of Prey*. New York: Facts On File, 1988. This book explains how birds of prey are useful to humans and wildlife and shows that raptors can be a joy to observe in the wild.

Emery and Durga Bernhard, *Eagles: Lions of the Sky*. New York: Holiday House, 1994. This colorfully illustrated text explores many aspects of eagle behavior, including courtship, mating, nest building, hunting, and the rearing of their young.

Michael Bright, *Project Wildlife: Eagles*. New York: Gloucester Press, 1990. Books in this series look at particular species in danger of extinction. The text of this book explains why eagles have become endangered and explores the efforts to save them for future generations.

Leslie Brown, *Eagles*. New York: Arco Publishing, 1970. For the slightly more advanced reader, this book offers a summary of the behavior of eagles throughout the world.

Karen Dudley, *The Untamed World: Bald Eagles.* Austin, TX: Raintree, 1998. The author of this book combines scientific facts, environmental concerns, and mythology and folklore to discuss the lifestyle of bald eagles.

Aubrey Lang, *Eagles.* New York: Econo-Clad Books, 1999. Color photographs and drawings illustrate different species of eagles from various countries. Hunting, eating behavior, and other topics are included in the text.

Glenda Powell Olsen, *Birds of Prey.* Chicago: Child's World, 1994. This text describes the physical characteristics of ospreys, falcons, vultures, eagles, and other types of birds of prey.

Peter Parnall, *The Daywatchers.* New York: Macmillan, 1984. The author of this book discusses American birds of prey and offers anecdotes about his experience with them. Eagles, hawks, ospreys, and falcons are included in the discussions.

Dorothy Hinshaw Patent, *Where the Bald Eagles Gather.* New York: Clarion, 1984. This photoessay book explores the lives of bald eagles as they gather at Glacier National Park in Montana. What attracts the eagles to the park, how scientists learn about the birds, and what is being done to protect eagles from humans are topics included for discussion.

————, *The Bald Eagle Returns*. New York: Clarion, 2000. The author describes how bald eagles have recovered from the threat of extinction, how they raise their families, and why they are the national bird of the United States.

Helen Roney Sattler, *The Book of Eagles*. New York: Lothrop, Lee & Shepard Books, 1989. Well known for her science writing, the author of this book explains the body structure, flight and hunting, and mating and nesting of eagles. The text is accompanied by lifelike color drawings of eagles and a glossary that describes all sixty species of the birds.

Stephen R. Swinburne, *In Good Hands: Behind the Scenes at a Center for Orphaned and Injured Birds*. San Francisco: Sierra Club Books for Children, 1998. This book provides a behind-the-scenes look at the Vermont Raptor Center, where volunteers rescue and rehabilitate hurt or abandoned birds of prey and eventually release them back into the wild.

Index

Picture Credits

Cover photo: © Jeff Vanuga/CORBIS
© ABPL/Dennis, Nigel / Animals/Animals Earth
  Scenes, 23
© AFP/CORBIS, 12
Corel, 14, 20, 22, 38
© Tim Fitzharris/Minden Pictures, 25
© Natalie Fobes/CORBIS, 18
© Gunter Max Photography/CORBIS, 35 (bot-
  tom)
© Lindsay Hebberd/CORBIS, 31
© Peter Johnson/CORBIS, 33 (bottom), 37
Chris Jouan, 6 and 7, 11 (bottom), 15 (right)
© Frans Lanting/Minden Pictures, 27
© OSF/AndrewArthaSurvival / Animals/Animals
  Earth Scenes, 28
PhotoDisc, 11 (top)
© D. Robert & Lorri Franz/CORBIS, 4
© Paul A. Souders/CORBIS, 33 (top)
© Kennan Ward/CORBIS, 15 (left)
© Adam Woolfitt/CORBIS, 35 (top)
© Konrad Wothe/Minden Pictures, 9

About the Author

Hayley Mitchell Haugen holds masters degrees in English and creative writing, and she is currently working on her Ph.D. in American literature at Ohio University. She teaches creative writing and composition at the college level and has written numerous nonfiction books for teens published by Greenhaven Press/Lucent Books.